Can You Find It Inside?

Can You Find It Inside?

Jessica Schulte

THE METROPOLITAN MUSEUM OF ART

Harry N. Abrams, Inc., Publishers

Published in 2005 by The Metropolitan Museum of Art, New York, and Harry N. Abrams, Incorporated, New York
Copyright © 2005 by The Metropolitan Museum of Art

First Edition
Printed in China
14 13 12 11 10 09 08 07 06 05   5 4 3 2 1

Produced by the Department of Special Publications, The Metropolitan Museum of Art:
Robie Rogge, Publishing Manager; Jessica Schulte, Project Editor; Anna Raff, Designer; Gillian Moran, Production Associate.
Photography by The Metropolitan Museum of Art Photograph Studio.

Visit the Museum's Web site: www.metmuseum.org

Library of Congress Cataloging-in-Publication Data

Schulte, Jessica.
   Can you find it inside? / by Jessica Schulte.— 1st ed.
      p. cm.
   Includes bibliographical references and index.
   ISBN 0-8109-5794-9 (alk. paper)
   1. Painting—Themes, motives. 2. Painting—Appreciation. 3. Art—New York (State)—New York. 4.
Metropolitan Museum of Art (New York, N.Y.) I. Metropolitan Museum of Art (New York, N.Y.) II. Title.
   ND1143.S36 2005
   759—dc22
                                                                    2005000990

ISBN 1-58839-138-8 (MMA)
ISBN 0-8109-5794-9 (Abrams)

Harry N. Abrams, Inc.
100 Fifth Avenue
New York, NY 10011
www.abramsbooks.com

Abrams is a subsidiary of

LA MARTINIÈRE
GROUPE

INTRODUCTION

Here are thirteen paintings from the collections of The Metropolitan Museum of Art that tell stories, hold surprises, and beckon the youngest readers to look again and again at each work of art.

Every painting in this book shows a different indoor scene that contains colorful details to pore over. Some of the scenes, like the one depicted in Fairfield Porter's *Lizzie at the Table*, show everyday routines that children will know, from playing games and taking naps to gathering for lunch.

Other scenes might seem a little unusual to children. Vermeer's *Woman with a Lute* features a winsome young woman playing an instrument not usually seen by children, while other works of art show children posing for formal portraits.

Each painting is accompanied by rhymes that guide readers, giving clues regarding the location of specific details. To keep the game going, there are even more objects to find listed at the bottom of the pages. But there's no reason for readers to stop there. They can keep searching to see what else might be "hidden" in the painting.

Youngsters will love being sent on a treasure hunt through art—the prize is in the looking!

—Jessica Schulte

If you look, don't make a peep.
You'll spy a baby fast asleep.

Do you see them? Now, don't blink!
Baby's shoes are small and pink.

Can you find it? It is there—
A bright blue ribbon in Mom's hair.

Keep looking. Can you also find a ball of yarn, silver buckles, and a bonnet?

Can you find it? Straight ahead,
A man is sitting, slicing bread.

Can you find it? Look and stare—
A cat sits by the rocking chair.

Look again, what do you see?
Mom holds baby lovingly.

Keep looking. Can you also
find a clock, some books,
and a basket of dishes?

Do you see it? Can you spot
A tall, black-handled coffeepot?

Glance around and if you look,
You will see a big fat book.

Search again and look anew.
Do you see the color blue?

Keep looking. Can you
also find a spoon, a high
chair, and an orange?

If you look this way and that,
You'll see a woman in a hat.

Look above, then look below,
And count the grapefruits in a row.

Can you find it? Can you spy?
A man at dinner wears a tie.

Keep looking. Can you
also find a cash register,
a basket, and pork chops?

Can you find a thing or four?
Three rackets raised, one on the floor.

If you look, with time and care,
You'll see a shuttlecock in midair.

Can you find them, can you spot
White flowers in a flowerpot?

Keep looking. Can you
also find sailboats,
chimneys, and a book?

If you look and if you gaze,
You'll see flowers in a vase.

Can you find a bright red shoe,
And then another one that's blue?

Can you find it? It's a sight!
An easel with a scene in white.

Keep looking. Can you
also find a red sash, a fancy
chair, and a pink rose?

Can you find it? Now, look sharp!
There's a lovely golden harp.

If you look at everything,
You might find two golden rings.

Can you find it? It's for certain,
There's a long green velvet curtain.

Keep looking. Can you
also find a blue tie, tassels,
and a little picture?

Can you find him? Look again.
A bearded man has a quill pen.

Do you hear it say *tick-tock*?
Can you find a wooden clock?

Can you spot them with your eye?
Ears of corn are hung to dry.

Keep looking. Can you also
find a book on the floor, a
candle, and children hiding?

Do you see—it's gone astray.
A little girl wants her bouquet.

Is it gone? Imagine that!
Can you find the fine straw hat?

Do you see them on the wall?
Golden frames, just count them all!

Keep looking. Can you also find antlers, a purple sash, and striped socks?

Take your time, go very slow.
Find gold buttons in a row.

Now speed up, go zoom, zoom, zoom!
Find a dog in the fancy room.

Look again, now don't be reckless.
Keep on searching. Find the necklace.

Keep looking. Can you also
find two ruffled collars, a long
blue sash, and a footstool?

Do you see the flowers on it?
Someone has a brand-new bonnet!

Gaze and see, then look some more—
Find three onions on the floor.

Can you look for something new?
Do you see a stripe that's blue?

Keep looking. Can you
also find a letter, an empty
hatbox, and a pumpkin?

Look around and be astute.
Can you find a tuneful lute?

It's so easy—it's a snap!
Look above and find a map.

Look way down, now just explore.
Find the squares upon the floor.

Keep looking. Can you also find
a black chair, a tablecloth, and a
windowpane with designs?

The works of art reproduced in this book are from the collections of The Metropolitan Museum of Art, unless otherwise noted.

The First Babe
Jehan Georges Vibert, French, 1840–1902
Watercolor on paper, 14⅛ x 17½ in., 1872
Catharine Lorillard Wolfe Collection, Bequest of
Catharine Lorillard Wolfe, 1887   87.15.8

Just Moved
Henry Mosler, American, 1841–1920
Oil on canvas, 29 x 36½ in., 1870
Arthur Hoppock Hearn Fund, 1962   62.80

Lizzie at the Table
Fairfield Porter, American,
1907–1975
Oil on canvas, 36½ x 45½ in., 1958
Bequest of Arthur M. Bullowa, 1993
1993.406.2

Tables for Ladies
Edward Hopper, American, 1882–1967
Oil on canvas, 48¼ x 60¼ in., 1930
George A. Hearn Fund, 1931   31.62

The Children of Nathan Starr
Ambrose Andrews, American, circa 1801–1877
Oil on canvas, 28⅛ x 36½ in., 1835
Gift of Nina Howell Starr, in memory of
Nathan Comfort Starr (1896–1981), 1987
1987.404

*Atelier of a Painter, Probably Madam
Vigée Le Brun (1755–1842) and Her Pupil*
Marie Victoire Lemoine, French, 1754–1820
Oil on canvas, 45⅛ x 35 in.
Gift of Mrs. Thorneycroft Ryle, 1957
57.103

The Music Lesson
John George Brown, American, 1831–1913
Oil on canvas, 24 x 20 in., 1870
Gift of Colonel Charles A. Fowler, 1921
21.115.3

*The Contest for the Bouquet: The
Family of Robert Gordon in Their New
York Dining Room*
Seymour Joseph Guy, American,
1824–1910
Oil on canvas, 24⅛ x 29½ in., 1866
Purchase, Gift of William E. Dodge,
by exchange, and Lila Acheson
Wallace Gift, 1992   1992.128

Taking the Census
Francis W. Edmonds,
American, 1806–1863
Oil on canvas, 28 x 38 in., 1854
Lent by Diane Wolf, Daniel Wolf, and Mathew Wolf

The Knapp Children
Samuel Lovett Waldo, American, 1783–1861;
William Jewett, American, 1792–1874
Oil on canvas, 70 x 57½ in., circa 1833–34
Gift of Mrs. John Knapp Hollins, in memory
of her husband, 1959   59.114

The New Bonnet
Francis W. Edmonds, American, 1806–1863
Oil on canvas, 25 x 30⅛ in., 1858
Purchase, Erving Wolf Foundation Gift and Gift of
Hanson K. Corning, by exchange, 1975   1975.27.1

Woman with a Lute
Johannes Vermeer, Dutch, 1632–1675
Oil on canvas, 20¼ x 18 in., early 1660s
Bequest of Collis P. Huntington, 1900   25.110.24

BACK JACKET
Conversation Piece
Lilly Martin Spencer, American, 1822–1902
Oil on canvas, 28⁵⁄₁₆ x 22⅝ in., circa 1851
Maria DeWitt Jesup and Morris K. Jesup Funds, 1998   1998.413